BLUEPRINTS

Maths
Key Stage 1
Copymasters

Wendy and David Clemson

Moresby School

Stanley Thornes (Publishers) Ltd

BLUEPRINTS – HOW TO GET MORE INFORMATION

The following titles are currently available. New titles are being added every year.

Topics
Assemblies
Writing
Science Key Stage 1 Teacher's Resource Book
Science Key Stage 1 Pupils' Copymasters
Science Key Stage 2 Teacher's Resource Book
Science Key Stage 2 Pupils' Copymasters
English Key Stage 1 Teacher's Resource Book
English Key Stage 1 Pupils' Copymasters
English Key Stage 2 Teacher's Resource Book
English Key Stage 2 Pupils' Copymasters
History Key Stage 1 Teacher's Resource Book
History Key Stage 1 Pupils' Copymasters
History Key Stage 2 Teacher's Resource Book
History Key Stage 2 Pupils' Copymasters
Environmental Education Key Stage 1
Environmental Education Key Stage 2

Geography Key Stage 1 Teacher's Resource Book
Geography Key Stage 1 Pupils' Copymasters
Geography Key Stage 2 Teacher's Resource Book
Geography Key Stage 2 Pupils' Copymasters
Technology Key Stage 1
Technology Key Stage 2
Health Education Key Stage 1 Teacher's Resource Book
Health Education Key Stage 1 Pupils' Copymasters
Health Education Key Stage 2 Teacher's Resource Book
Health Education Key Stage 2 Pupils' Copymasters
Maths Key Stage 1 Teacher's Resource Book
Maths Key Stage 1 Pupils' Copymasters
Maths Key Stage 2 Teacher's Resource Book
Maths Key Stage 2 Pupils' Copymasters

Books may be bought by credit card over the telephone and information obtained on (0242) 228888. Alternatively, photocopy and return this FREEPOST form for further information.

Photocopiable

Please send further information on BLUEPRINTS to:

Name _____

Address_____

_____

Postcode_____

To: Marketing Services Dept., Stanley Thornes Publishers, FREEPOST (GR 782), Cheltenham, Glos. GL53 1BR

Applications for such permission should be addressed to the publishers:
Stanley Thornes (Publishers) Ltd, Old Station Drive, Leckhampton, CHELTENHAM GL53 0DN, England.

First published in 1992 by:
Stanley Thornes (Publishers) Ltd
Old Station Drive
Leckhampton
CHELTENHAM GL53 0DN

British Library Cataloguing in Publication Data

A catalogue record for this book is available from the British Library.

ISBN 07487 1169 4

Typeset by Tech-Set, Gateshead, Tyne & Wear
Printed in Great Britain at The Bath Press, Avon

CONTENTS

INTRODUCTION

In this book there are 115 photocopiable worksheets. C1–C103 are linked specifically to activities in the *Teacher's Resource Book*. C104 is a teacher record sheet. R1–R11 are so called because they are resource copymasters and are intended for use again and again across all sections of the book. Where the photocopy sheets are referred to in the text of the *Teacher's Resource Book* there are some instructions on how to use them. They are referred to by number in the *Teacher's Resource Book* by this symbol:

When the children have completed these worksheets they can be added to workfiles or used as exemplar material in pupil profiles. You may also wish to use completed worksheets as a resource for your assessments. There is a tick list on copymaster C104, on which you can note the photocopy sheets the children have used.

Numeral–set match

Match

1

2

3

4

5

6

Counting and recording counts

How many?

Counting and recording counts

How many?

eyes ☐

ears ☐

noses ☐

mouths ☐

faces ☐

eyebrows ☐

Counting and recording counts

How many?

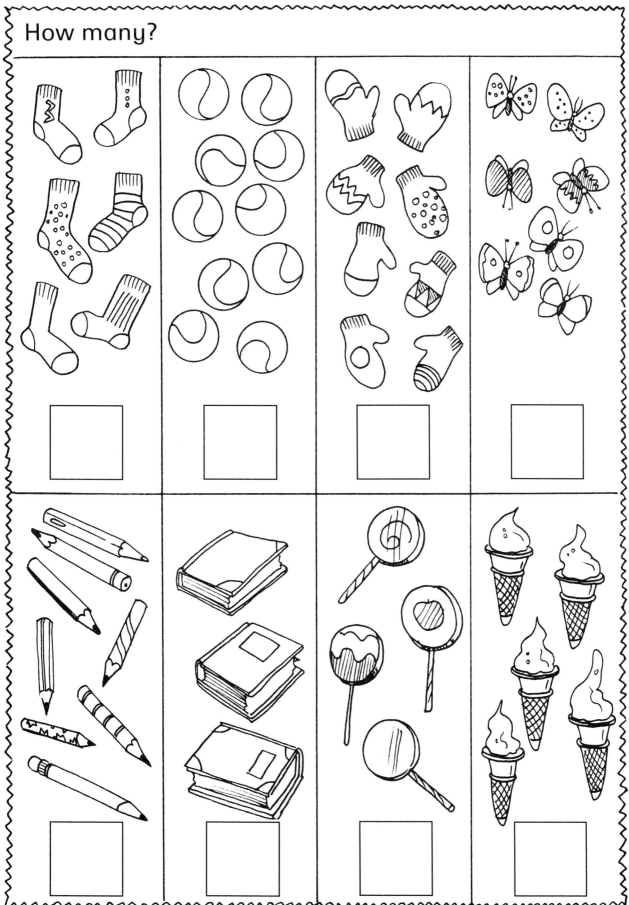

Pairs

How many pairs?

pair of eyes

pair of ears

pair of lips

pair of hands

pair of arms

pair of legs

pair of feet

pair of socks

pair of trainers

Ordinal numbers

Who will win the race?

Write 1st 2nd 3rd by the cars

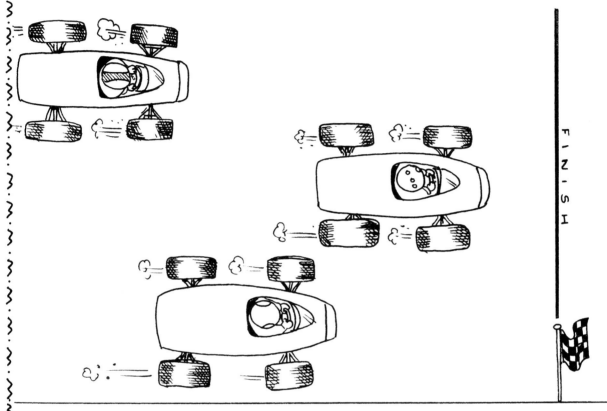

Match

second   fourth   third   first

3rd   1st   4th   2nd

Conservation of 5

Colour and count

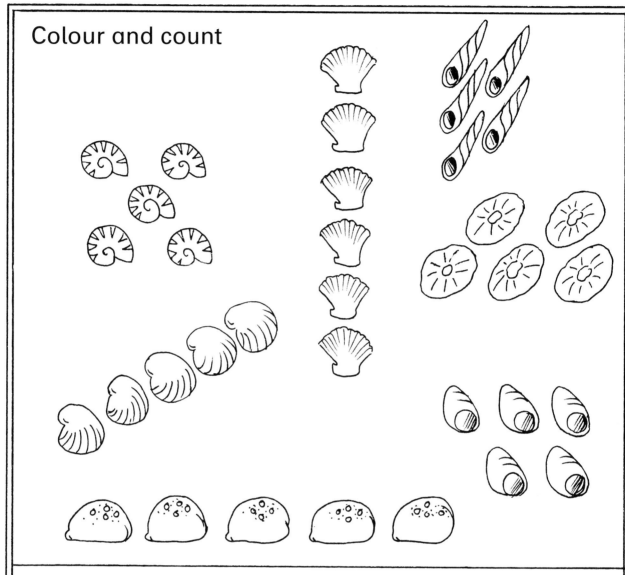

Draw more patterns of 5

Conservation of 2, 3, 5

Colour groups of 2 red, 3 blue and 5 green

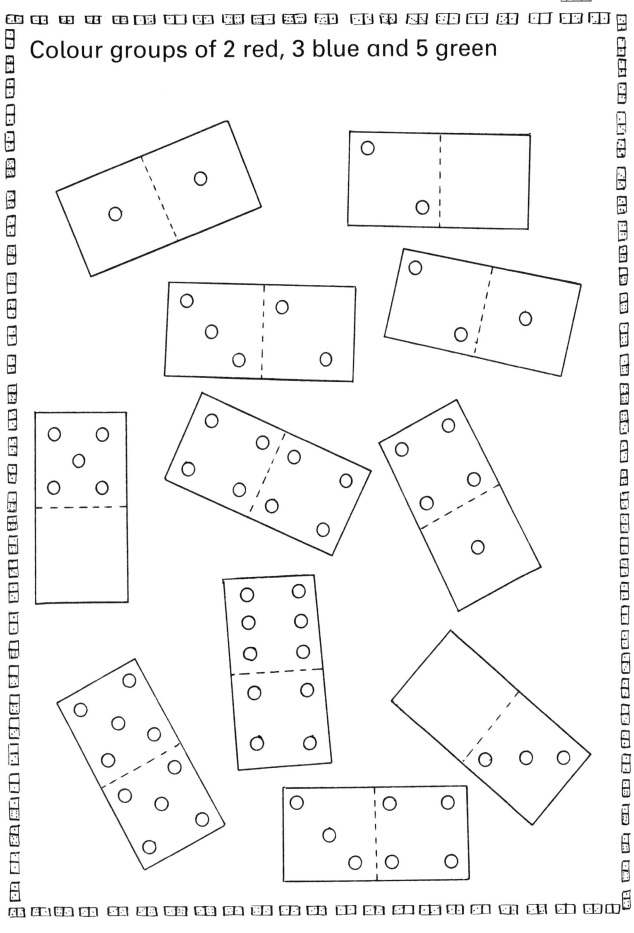

Ladybird race

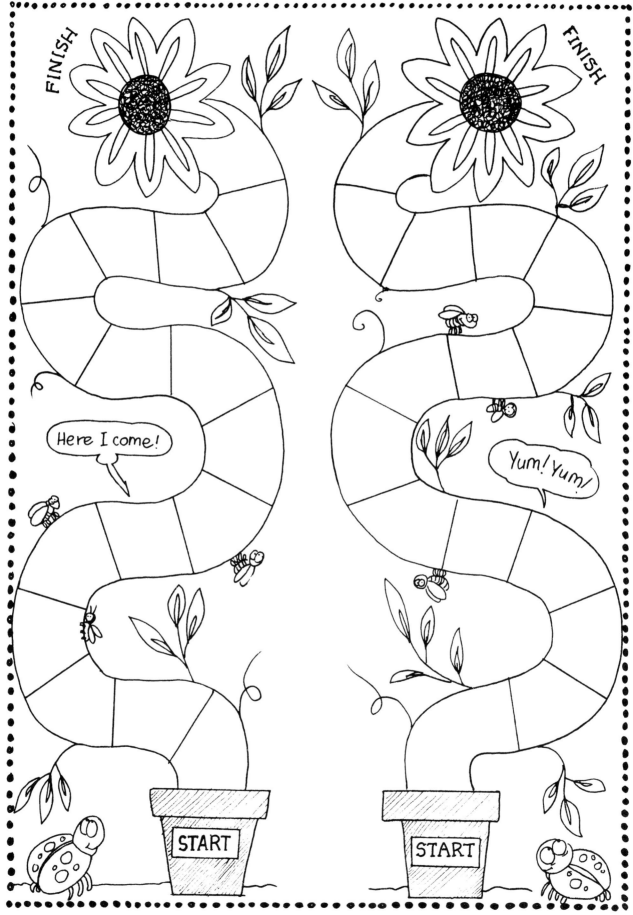

Cheese chase

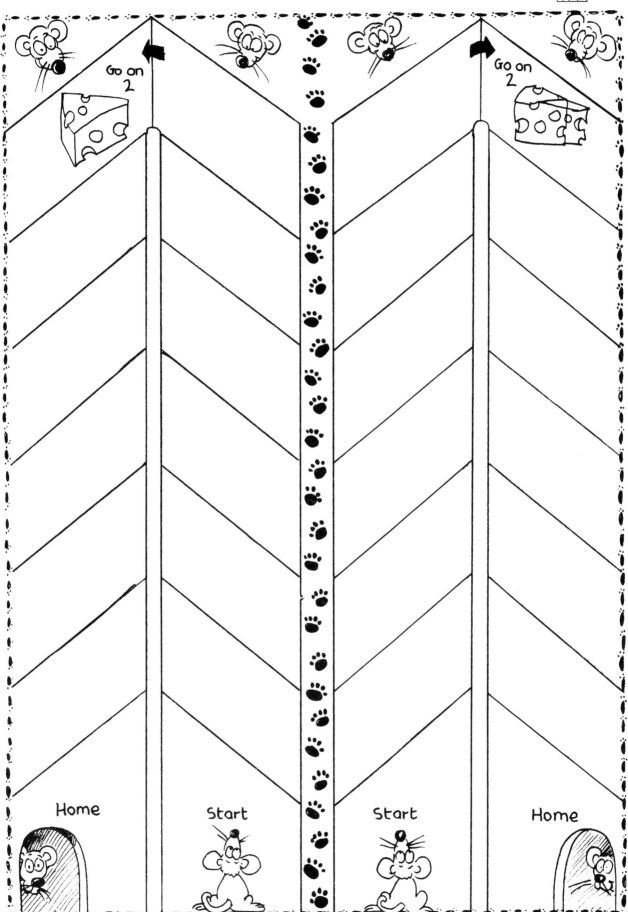

Home-time!

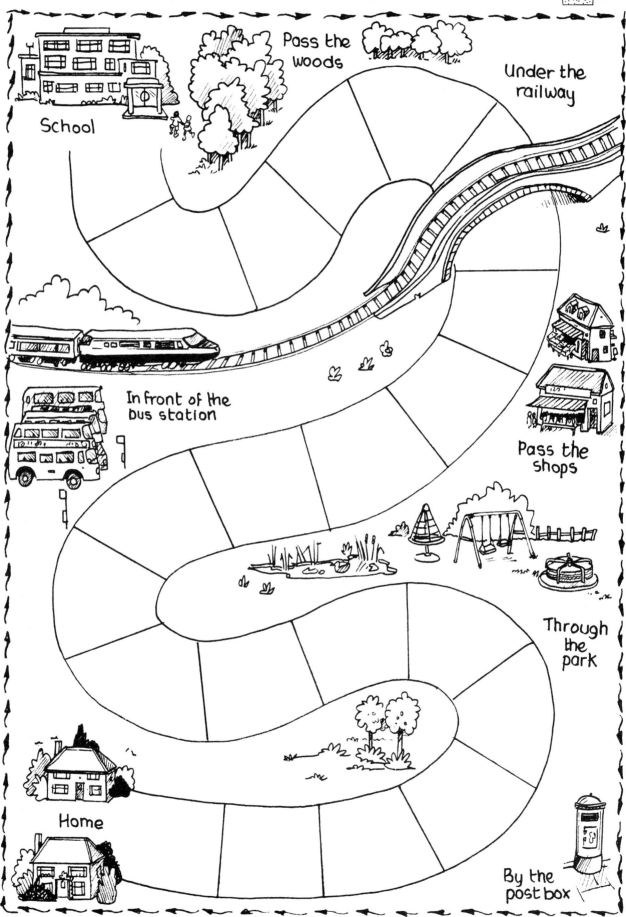

Aliens

Take away strips

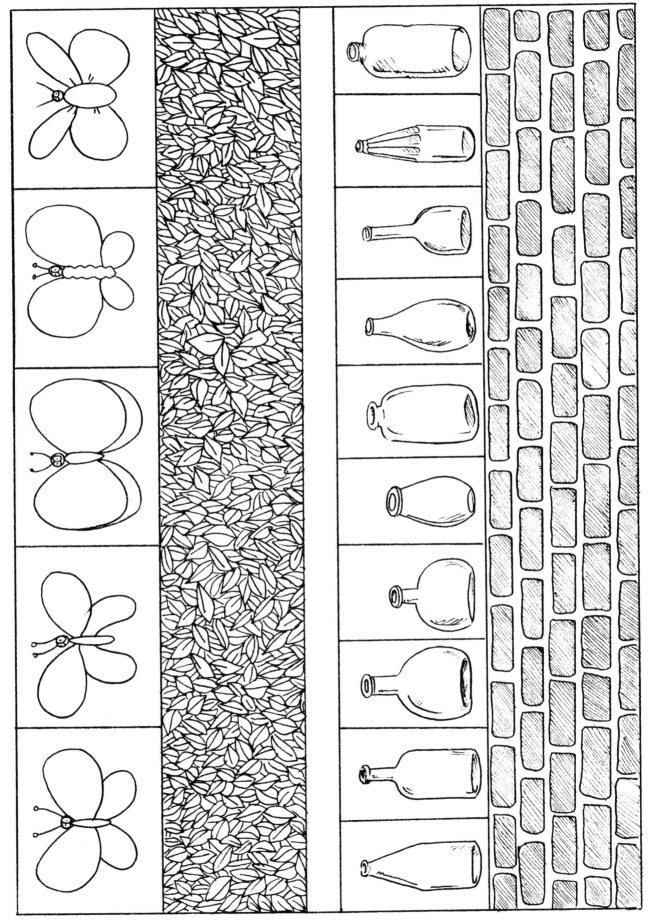

Leap frog

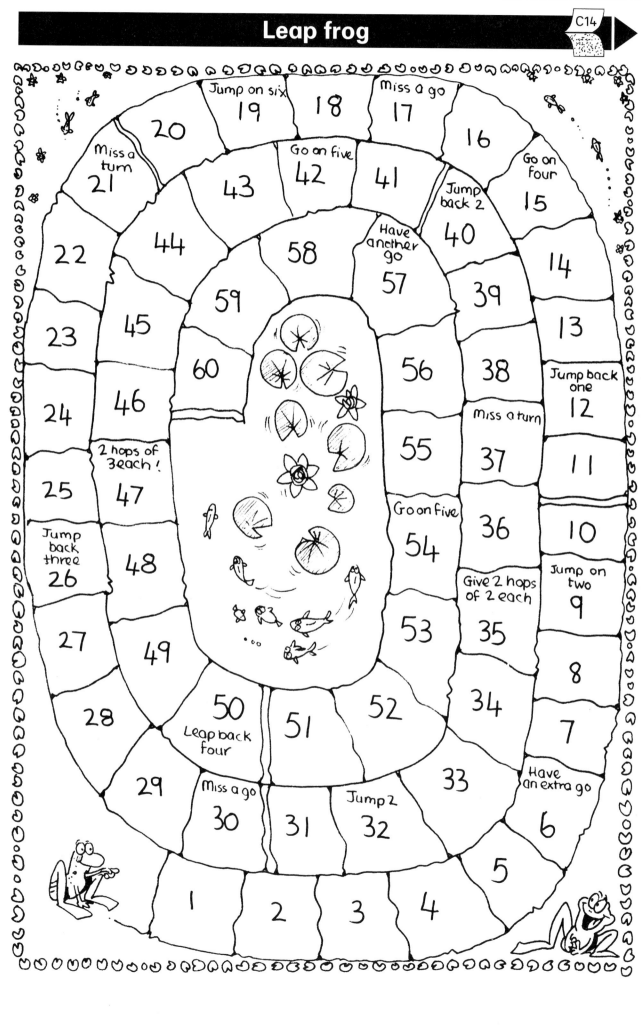

Planes and parachutes

Finish 100	99	98	Down you go 97	96	95	94	93	92	91
81	82	83	84	85	86	87	88	89	90
80	79	78	Down you go 77	76	75	74	73 Take off	72	71
61	62	63	64	65	66	Down you go 67	68	69	70
60 Take off	59	58	57	56	55	54	53	52	51
41	42	43	44	45	46	47 Take off	Down you go 48	49	50
40	39	38	37	36	35	34	33	32	31
21	22	23	24	25	26	27	28 Take off	29	Down you go 30
20	19 Take off	18	17	16	15	14	13	12	11
1 Start	2	3 Take off	4	5 Take off	6	7	8	9	10

Make five

1	(pencil)	2	(ladybirds)	3	(clouds)	5	(flowers)
1	(shoe)	2	(fish)	2	(bottles)	2	(tadpoles)
(hat)	1	2	(ice creams)	3	(sweets)	3	(swords)
1	(cookie)	1	(pot)	1	(snail)	5	(ice lollies)
(onion)	1	1	(mouse)	1	(cherry)	5	(beans)
(bananas)	3	1	(butterfly)	1	(heart)	1	(rabbit)
2	(socks)	3	(snails)	1	(spade)	1	(rabbit)
1	(balloon)	1	(basket)	2	(bins)	4	(mittens)
4	(circles)	1	(mug)	1	(sweet)	1	(pig)

Make ten

C17

9	1	⊞ 8 ⊞	2
7	3	6	4
5	5	4	6
5	5	3	7
2	⊞ 8 ⊞	9	1
2	3	5	4
1	5	6	3
1	⊞ 8 ⊞	1	1
7	2	1	9

Add and subtract

10 − 3 →

7 − 1 →

5 − 2 →

8 − 4 →

9 − 5 →

2 − 1 →

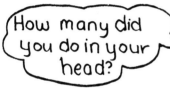

How many did you do in your head?

I am a good adder!

4 + 2 →

4 + 6 →

7 − 3 →

7 + 3 →

5 + 5 →

10 − 5 →

9 − 6 →

What is missing?

7 − ▢ → 4

4 + ▢ → 8

6 + ▢ → 10

▢ + 2 → 5

▢ + 5 → 7

▢ + 3 → 9

Put in the sign + or −?

5   5 → 10

6   2 → 4

7   2 → 9

3   2 → 5

6 → 3   3

5 → 8   3

4 → 2   2

Equivalence

Join those of equal value

Change

I spend	I pay	My change is
10p	20p	10p
12p	15p	
2p	5p	
11p	15p	
6p	7p	
3p	5p	
1p	5p	
4p	10p	
12p	20p	
14p	15p	
5p	10p	
7p	10p	
13p	20p	

Halves

Ring a half (½) of these

kite	
pear	
lolly	
egg	
piece of paper	

Quarters

Ring a quarter ($\frac{1}{4}$) of these

orange

cheese sandwich

flag

cherry cake

Exciting things to measure with

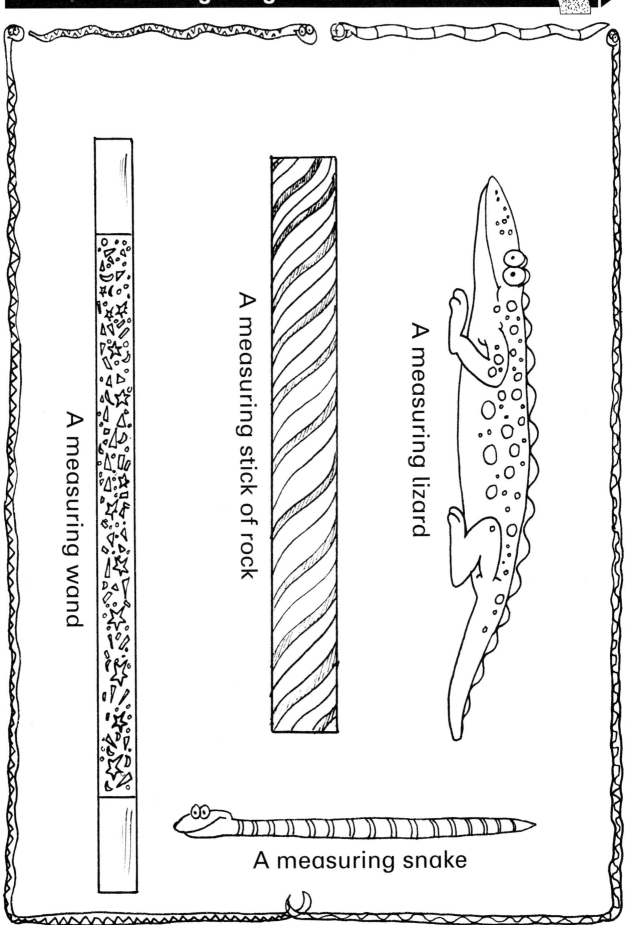

A measuring wand

A measuring stick of rock

A measuring lizard

A measuring snake

Measuring: non-standard units

C24

Draw what you measure	Measure with:	How many?
	handspans	
	strides	
	thumbs	
	books	
	pencils	

Capacity

Get four containers of different sizes

Label them

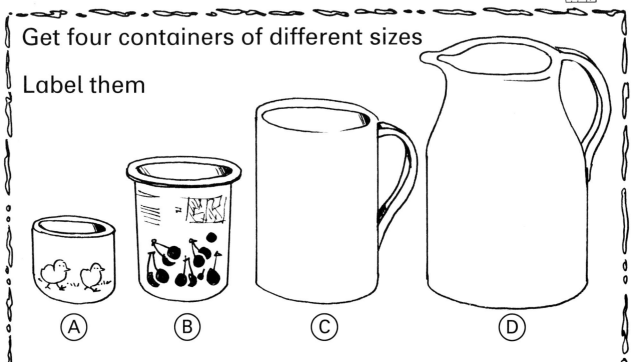

A   B   C   D

How many?

☐ (A) fill 1 (B)   ☐ (B) fill 1 (C)

☐ (A) fill 1 (C)   ☐ (B) fill 1 (D)

☐ (A) fill 1 (D)   ☐ (C) fill 1 (D)

Do some more using another container

Tens and units

C26

Set these out as tens and units

14   27   74   32   46

Look for the pattern

15   25   35   45   55

Which is the biggest number
in these?

19   11   39   91   48

These are easy if you know the pattern

10   20   30   40   50

Thousands, hundreds, tens and units

Set these out as hundreds, tens and units

100   105   150   151   501

Try this for size! You need a thousands column

4321

Do these in order of size. Start with the smallest

122   5011   36   95   14

These numbers make a pattern

250   500   750   1000   1250

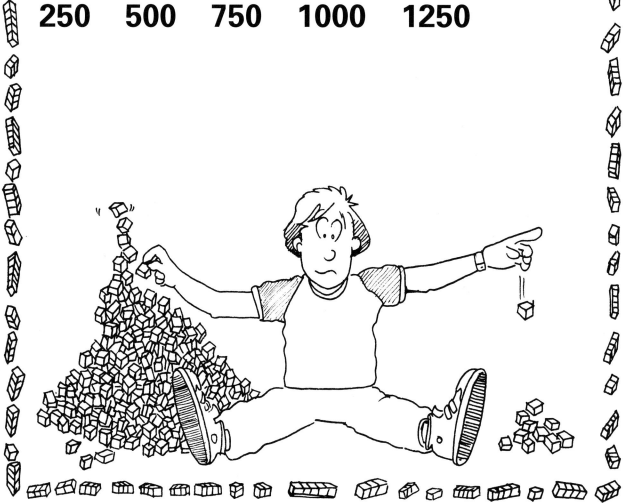

Big numbers in words

Write these in numerals

Subtraction bonds to 20

20 − 10	20 − 5	20 − 0	20 − 20

Join up like this

20   10   0   15

20 − 8	20 − 6	20 − 4	20 − 2

18   14   16   12

20 − 18	20 − 16	20 − 14	20 − 12

4   2   6   8

20 − 19	20 − 17	20 − 15	20 − 13

5   1   3   7

20 − 11	20 − 9	20 − 7	20 − 3

11   9   17   13

Bingo

C30

Base cards

17 − 11	10 − 5	4 + 2
7 + 8	13 − 3	10 + 10

5 − 5	18 − 7	9 + 5
7 − 3	14 + 2	12 + 8

19 − 7	15 − 5	8 + 2
5 − 0	16 + 3	8 + 9

20 − 10	9 − 6	17 − 9
4 + 12	8 − 5	10 − 10

Numerals

6	5	6	0	11	14
15	10	20	4	16	20
12	10	10	10	3	8
5	19	17	16	3	0

Missing numbers

0, 2, _____, 6, 8, _____, _____, 14, 16, _____, 20

0, 3, 6, _____, _____, 15, 18, 21, _____, _____, _____

0, 4, _____, 12, _____, 20, _____, 28, _____, 36, _____

0, 5, 10, _____, _____, _____, 30, 35, 40, _____, _____

0, 6, _____, 18, _____, 30, _____, 42, 54, 60

0, 7, 14, _____, _____, 35, _____, _____, 56, _____, 70

0, 8, _____, _____, 32, 40, _____, _____, 64, 72, _____

0, 9, _____, 27, 36, _____, _____, 63, 72, _____, 90

0, 10, _____, _____, _____, 50, 60, 70, _____, _____, _____

What's next in the pattern?

9, 12, 15, _____   35, 42, _____   60, 70, _____

10, 12, _____   20, 25, _____   8, 16, _____

Zap!

Multiply cards for Zap

1 × 2	2 × 2	3 × 2	4 × 2
5 × 2	6 × 2	7 × 2	8 × 2
9 × 2	10 × 2	1 × 3	3 × 3
4 × 3	5 × 3	6 × 3	7 × 3
8 × 3	9 × 3	10 × 3	1 × 5
4 × 5	5 × 5	6 × 5	7 × 5
8 × 5	9 × 5	10 × 5	1 × 10
4 × 10	6 × 10	7 × 10	8 × 10
9 × 10	10 × 10		

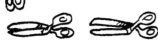

Multiplication ladders

×2	0 × 2 = 0
	1 × 2 =
	2 × 2 =
	3 × 2 =
	4 × 2 =
	5 × 2 =
	6 × 2 =
	7 × 2 =
	8 × 2 =
	9 × 2 =
	10 × 2 =

×3	0 × 3 = 0
	1 × 3 =
	2 × 3 =
	3 × 3 =
	4 × 3 =
	5 × 3 =
	6 × 3 =
	7 × 3 =
	8 × 3 =
	9 × 3 =
	10 × 3 =

×5	0 × 5 = 0
	1 × 5 =
	2 × 5 =
	3 × 5 =
	4 × 5 =
	5 × 5 =
	6 × 5 =
	7 × 5 =
	8 × 5 =
	9 × 5 =
	10 × 5 =

×10	0 × 10 = 0
	1 × 10 =
	2 × 10 =
	3 × 10 =
	4 × 10 =
	5 × 10 =
	6 × 10 =
	7 × 10 =
	8 × 10 =
	9 × 10 =
	10 × 10 =

C34

Picture sharing

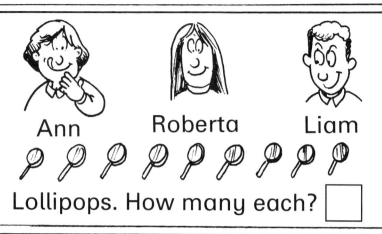

Lollipops. How many each? ☐

Honey pots. How many each? ☐

Worms. How many each? ☐

Cherries. How many each? ☐

Division puzzles

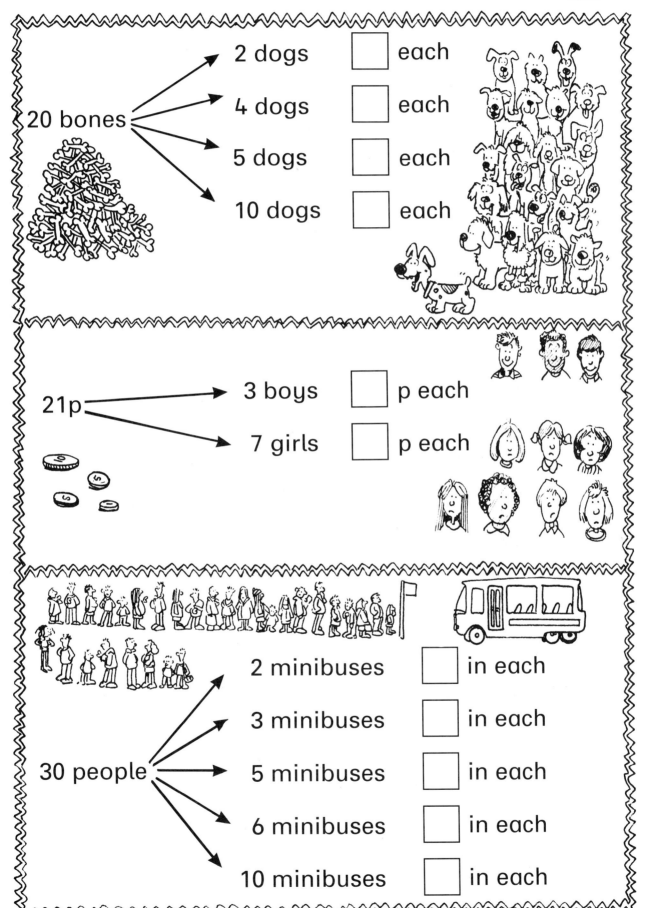

20 bones

2 dogs [ ] each

4 dogs [ ] each

5 dogs [ ] each

10 dogs [ ] each

21p

3 boys [ ] p each

7 girls [ ] p each

30 people

2 minibuses [ ] in each

3 minibuses [ ] in each

5 minibuses [ ] in each

6 minibuses [ ] in each

10 minibuses [ ] in each

Divide cards for Zap

2 ÷ 4	4 ÷ 2	6 ÷ 2	8 ÷ 2
10 ÷ 2	12 ÷ 2	14 ÷ 2	16 ÷ 2
18 ÷ 2	20 ÷ 2	3 ÷ 3	6 ÷ 3
9 ÷ 3	12 ÷ 3	15 ÷ 3	18 ÷ 3
21 ÷ 3	24 ÷ 3	27 ÷ 3	30 ÷ 3
5 ÷ 5	10 ÷ 5	15 ÷ 5	20 ÷ 5
25 ÷ 5	30 ÷ 5	35 ÷ 5	40 ÷ 5
45 ÷ 5	50 ÷ 5	10 ÷ 10	50 ÷ 10
100 ÷ 10			

Calculator checks

Check these using a calculator

Give a tick for correct answers
Cross out wrong answers
Write in the correct answer

$4 \times 3 = 12$

$27 \div 9 = 3$

$7 \times 8 = 56$

$60 \div 10 = 6$

$6 \times 7 = 42$

$7 - 5 = 2$

$50 - 10 = 40$

$44 - 11 = 41$

$100 \div 10 = 11$

$4 + 14 = 18$

Check these

$5 + 2 = 8$

$4 \times 4 = 16$

$7 \times 9 = 63$

$49 = 7 \times 7$

$63 = 9 \times 8$

$25 + 35 = 60$

$3 \times 11 = 30$

$24 = 20 + 5$

$80 = 10 \times 8$

$16 + 4 = 20$

Tickets, bills and receipts

A supermarket receipt

	£
Catfood	0.29
Catfood	0.26
Red apples	1.98
Pk. sausages	1.09
Peas	0.79
Fresh chicken	4.12
New potatoes	0.66
Mild cheddar	0.65
Rasp. yogurt	1.03
Balance due	9.87
Cash	10.00
Change	0.13

A bus ticket

A rail ticket

£5,05

Price tags

Bar code

95p

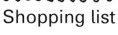

Jones the Papers
6, High Street, Newtown
Longshire LN9 PP9

DELIVERY ADDRESS
Williams
72 Lower Lane
Newton Longshire

INVOICE
NUMBER 1073

	£	
Newspapers 14th July to 25th August	25	95
Delivery charge	1	00
Total Due	26	95

Shopping list

Bill

Money problems

C40

Robin has 52p. She buys

She has ☐ left.

HAPPY BIRTHDAY 39p

CHOCCIE 12p

34p please

25p fine for late books

How much did he spend altogether?

Joan has 50p.

She gives 15p to her sister.

She puts 15p in her piggy bank.

She spends the rest.

How much does she spend?

Cherry cake 14p   Sausage roll 23p   Apple turnover 19p

You have 60p to spend. You may buy more than one of each. Draw what you could have and write how much change you would get.

change ☐   change ☐   change ☐

Shopping – track

START HERE →

Shopping lists

Toys. Buy these in the toy shop or post office.

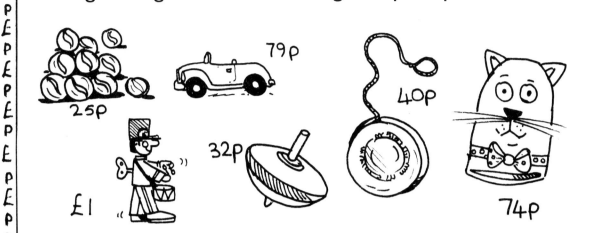

79p
25p
40p
32p
£1
74p

Stationery. Buy these in the toy shop or post office.

12p
£1.30
56p
25p
37p
90p

Sweets. Buy these in the sweet shop or post office.

55p
25p
39p
15p
11p
£2.05

Examples with some negative numbers

C43

20 + 0 = ☐   9 + 4 = ☐   11 − 15 = ☐

17 − 7 = ☐   5 − 8 = ☐

8 − 9 = ☐

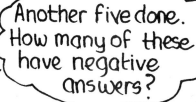

Six done! Three have negative answers.

4 − 5 = ☐   3 + 6 = ☐

10 − 5 = ☐   6 − 7 = ☐

12 + 6 = ☐

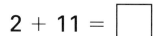

Another five done. How many of these have negative answers?

2 + 11 = ☐   ☐ = 9 + 9

13 + 5 = ☐   ☐ = 9 − 11

7 − 10 = ☐   ☐ = 8 − 2

Measuring in centimetres

Measure in centimetres

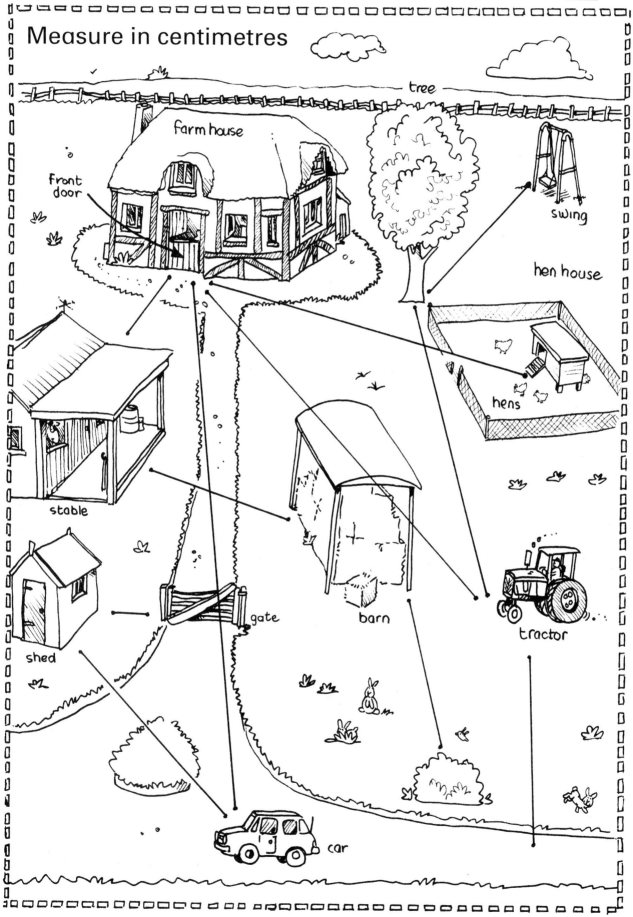

Litres and millilitres

There are _____ millilitres in a litre.

A cup full of tea has _____ ml.

A milk bottle holds _____ ml.

Find some more containers.
Draw them and write on the drawings
what they hold.

Clock face

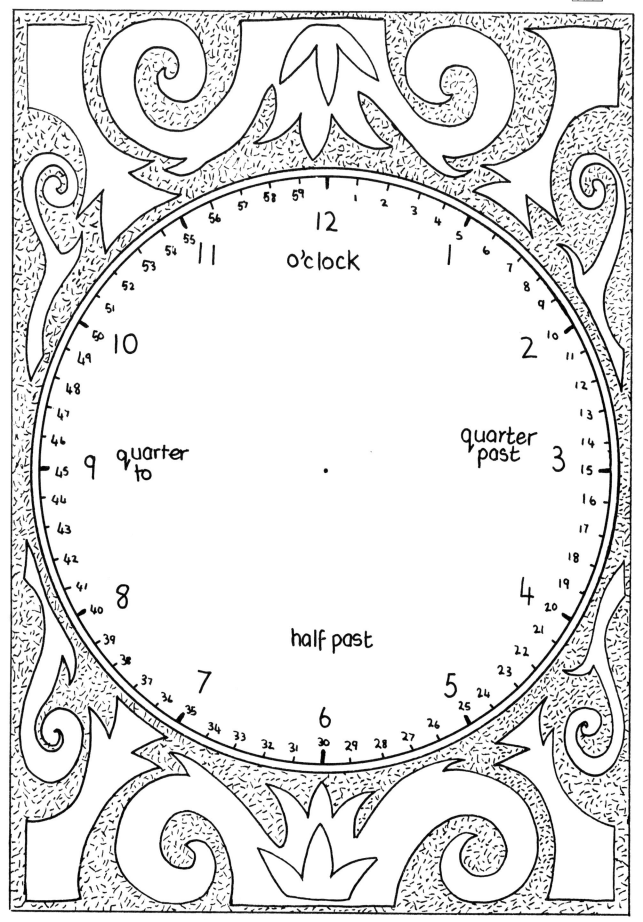

Telling the time

What is the time?

The long hand has fallen off these clocks.
Can you still tell the time?

What time will these clocks show 1 hour later?

Digital/written time

Turn these into digital times

four o'clock

half past two

quarter past ten

quarter to one

Write these times in words

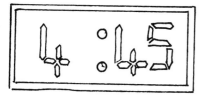

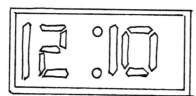

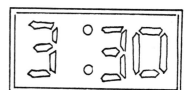

_____

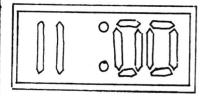

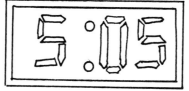

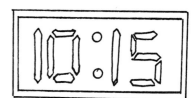

_____

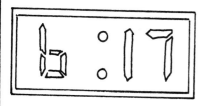

_____

Time

Put in the hands

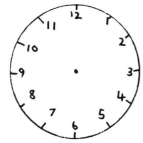
5 o'clock

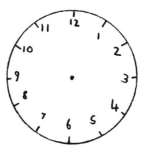
12 o'clock

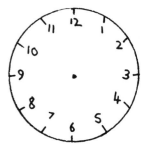
9 o'clock

Write in the time

_____   _____   _____

What is the difference in time between these clocks?

_____   _____

The long hand has fallen off. What is the time?

_____   _____   _____

Patterns around you

Can you find these patterns in things around you?

Where? Draw or write.

121212

Number patterns

Continue the patterns. Then play and check.

1 2 3 1 2 3 _____

4 6 4 6 4 6 _____

3 5 1 3 5 1 _____

7 2 7 2 7 2 _____

5 1 5 1 _____

6 2 6 2 _____

2 3 2 3 _____

7 3 7 3 1 7 3 7 3 1 _____

5 4 3 8 5 4 3 8 _____

1 2 1 3 1 2 1 3 _____

1 2 3 4 5 1 2 3 4 5 _____

Number bonds

C52

Make 5	Make 2	Make 3	Make 4
0 + 5	0 + 2	0 + 3	0 + 4
1 +	1 +	1 +	1 +
2 +	2 +	2 +	2 +
3 +		3 +	3 +
4 +	**Make 5**		4 +
5 +	10 −	**Make 7**	
	9 −	10 −	**Make 6**
Make 10	8 −	9 −	10 −
0 + 10	7 −	8 −	9 −
1 +	6 −	7 −	8 −
2 +	5 −		7 −
3 +		**Make 7**	6 −
4 +	**Make 5**	− 0	
5 +	− 0	− 1	**Make 6**
6 +	− 1	− 2	− 0
7 +	− 2	− 3	− 1
8 +	− 3		− 2
9 +	− 4		− 3
10 +	− 5		− 4

Odds and evens

Write in – odd or even

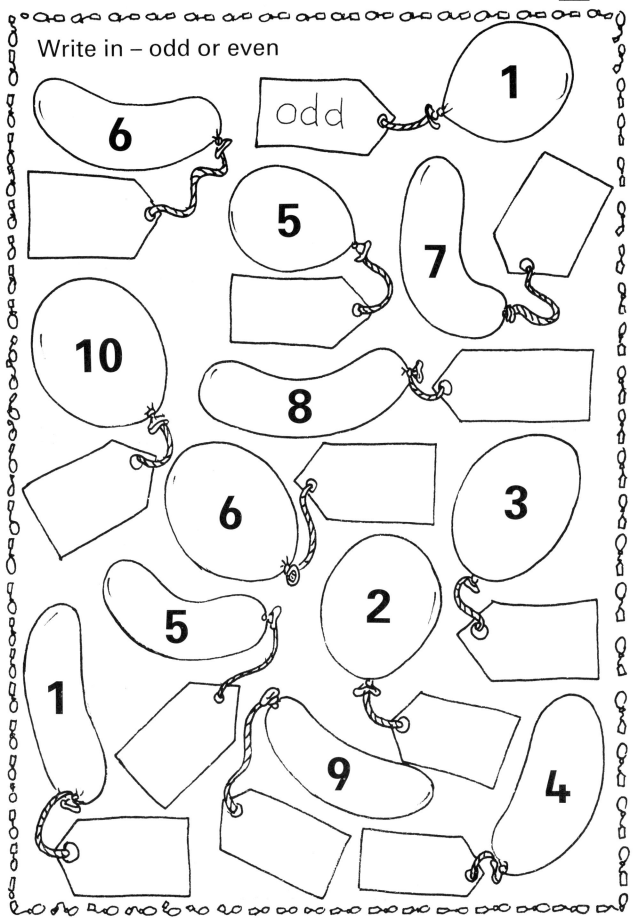

Prize winning numbers

Colour the numbers that win a prize

C55

Missing number mysteries

Find the missing numbers

$5 + \quad = 8$

$7 + \quad = 10$

$4 + \quad = 6$

$\quad + 4 = 8$

$\quad + 1 = 3$

$3 - \quad = 2$

$7 - \quad = 6$

$2 - \quad = 1$

$\quad - 5 = 5$

$\quad - 7 = 1$

$5 + \quad = 9$

$2 + \quad = 4$

$3 + \quad = 9$

$\quad + 5 = 6$

$\quad + 2 = 7$

$8 - \quad = 5$

$9 - \quad = 7$

$\quad - 4 = 3$

$\quad - 2 = 8$

$\quad - 1 = 3$

An add 3 robot

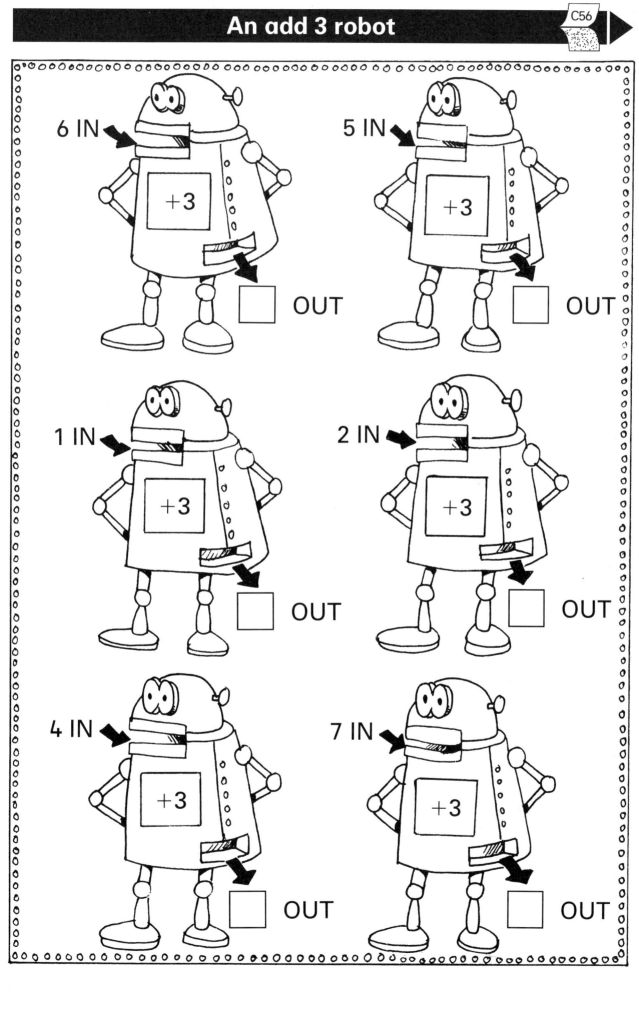

A take away 2 machine

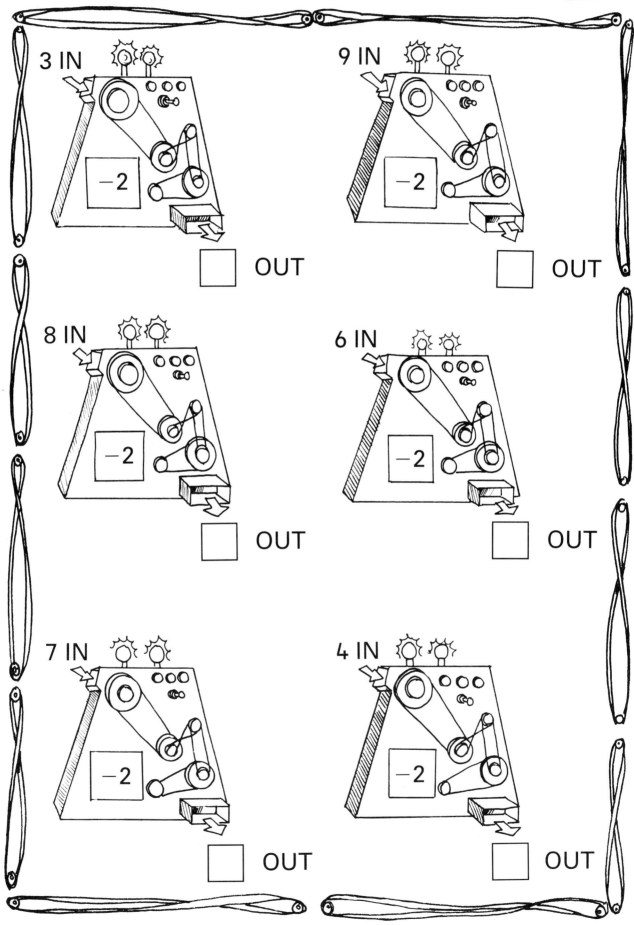

3 IN -2 ☐ OUT

9 IN -2 ☐ OUT

8 IN -2 ☐ OUT

6 IN -2 ☐ OUT

7 IN -2 ☐ OUT

4 IN -2 ☐ OUT

Computation trail

Start

Finish

5

Down the Well $+2$

Through the tunnel -5

Over the bridge

$+4$

$+8$

Across the river

$+5$

Up the tower

-1 Into the caves

-3

Through the swamp

On the train -7

$+6$

Up the mountain -4

Over the forest

Tens and units: addition

Work out the sums in this space

13 + 21

Answers

25 + 62

44 + 37

90 + 9

14 + 73

Tens and units: subtraction

Show what you do to get the answers

		Answers
64 − 13		
75 − 22		
38 − 15		
99 − 41		
50 − 25		

Add and subtract with approximation steps

C61

Work out rough answers
to these

41 + 31	
69 + 22	
78 − 32	
51 + 39	
29 + 48	
61 − 20	

Now use your calculator to check.

write your calculator answers here.

Number arrays

Continue the patterns

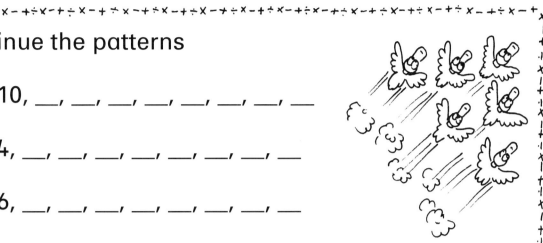

0, 5, 10, __, __, __, __, __, __, __, __

0, 2, 4, __, __, __, __, __, __, __, __

0, 3, 6, __, __, __, __, __, __, __, __

0, 10, 20, __, __, __, __, __, __, __, __

2 + 10 = 12	90 − 10 = 80
12 + 10 =	80 − 10 =
22 + 10 =	70 − 10 =
32 + 10 =	60 − 10 =

What is missing?

30, 35, 40, __, __, 55, __, __, __

24, 26, __, __, __, 34, 36, __, __

42, 45, 48, __, __, __, __

100, 90, __, __, __, __, __, __

27, 24, 21, __, __, __, __, __

20, 18, 16, __, __, __, __, __, __

An add 5 rocket

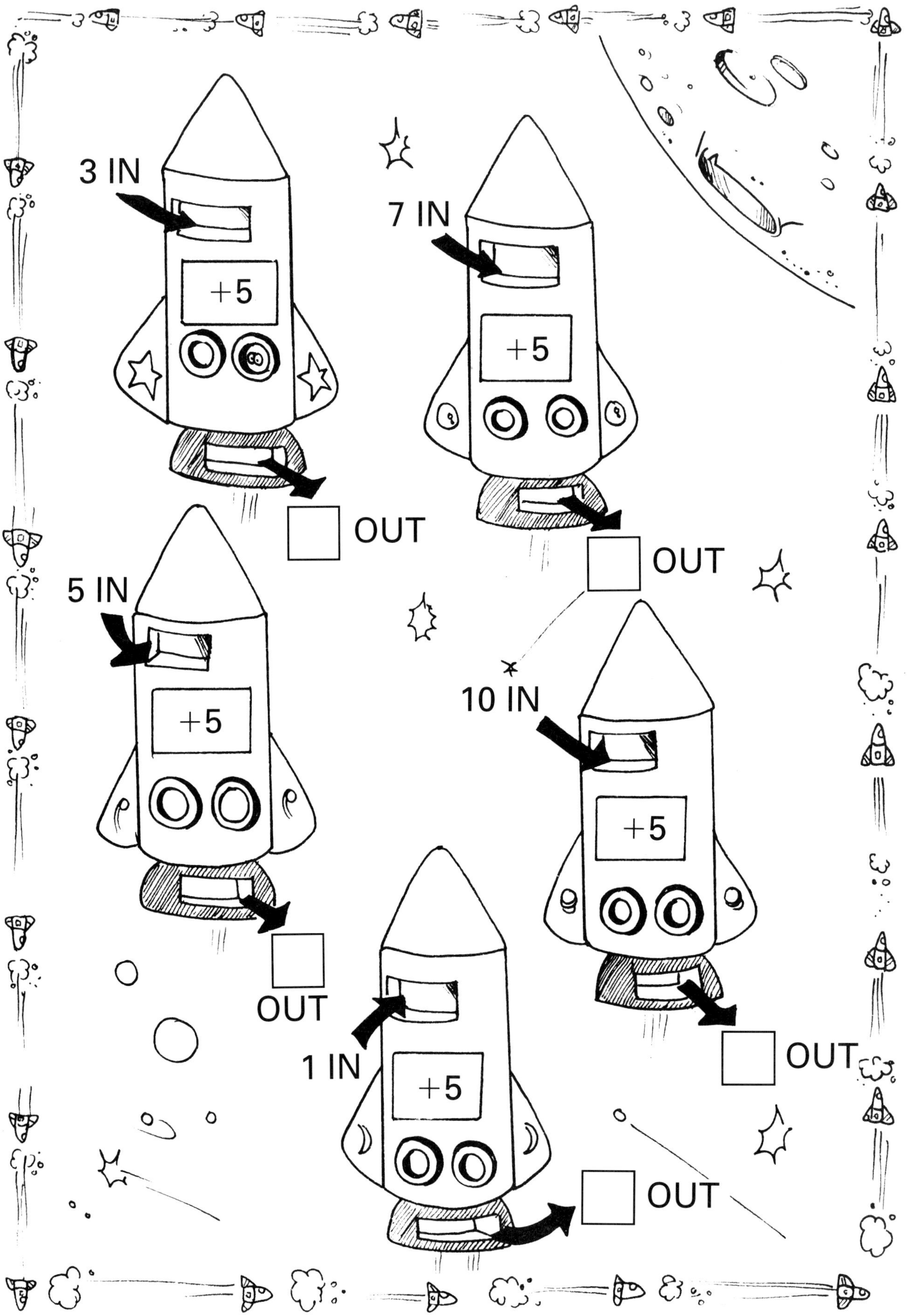

3 IN

+5

☐ OUT

7 IN

+5

☐ OUT

5 IN

+5

☐ OUT

10 IN

+5

☐ OUT

1 IN

+5

☐ OUT

A take away 7 machine

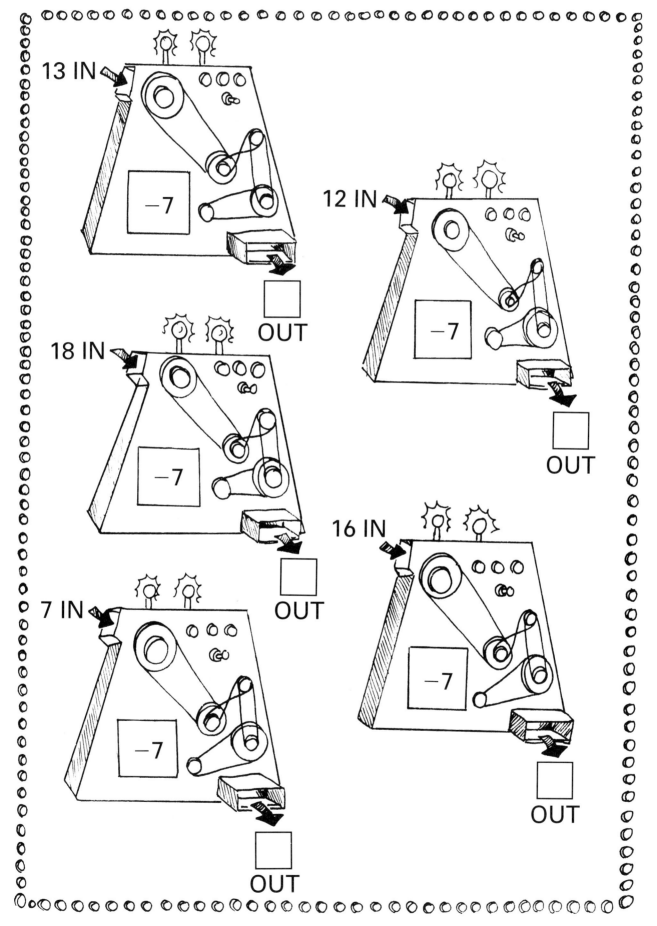

Star wars machines

Follow the trail

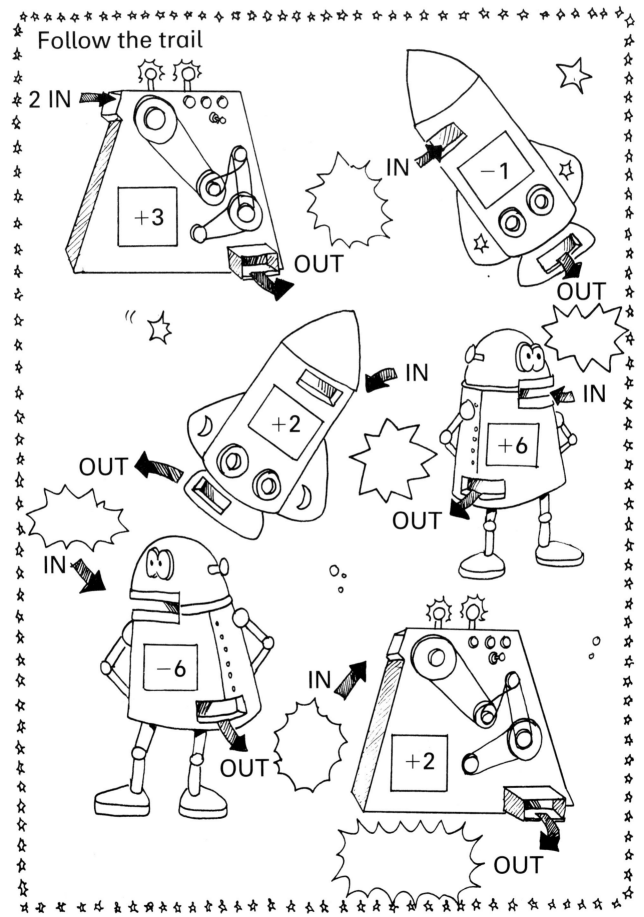

2 IN +3 OUT

IN −1 OUT

IN +2 OUT

IN +6 OUT

IN −6 OUT

IN +2 OUT

Mystery machines

What do these machines do?

9 IN

÷

OUT 3

3 IN

×

OUT 12

4 IN

+

OUT 10

5 IN

−

OUT 1

11 IN

−

OUT 6

5 IN

÷

OUT 1

Shape pictures

Draw a man of ◯ and ▭

Draw a kite of △

Draw a dog of ☐ and △

Draw a house of ☐ and ▭

Position words

Ring the correct words

under / on

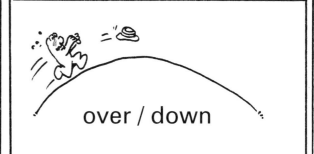
over / down

under / up

down / above

beside / above

on / under

beside / on

up / in front of

behind / over

on / down

above / under

Measuring vocabulary

C69

Ring these

2 4 6

Highest number

Smallest drum

Youngest child

Biggest door

Lightest

Fattest fish

Comparing measurements

Draw yourself and two friends

| Me | My friend | My friend |

_____   _____   _____

Draw and write.

Hand   _____ has the biggest hand.

Coat   _____ has the biggest coat.

Pet/Toy   _____ has the smallest pet/toy.

Restaurant comments

Draw what you ate and drank

Write about the food

Shape match

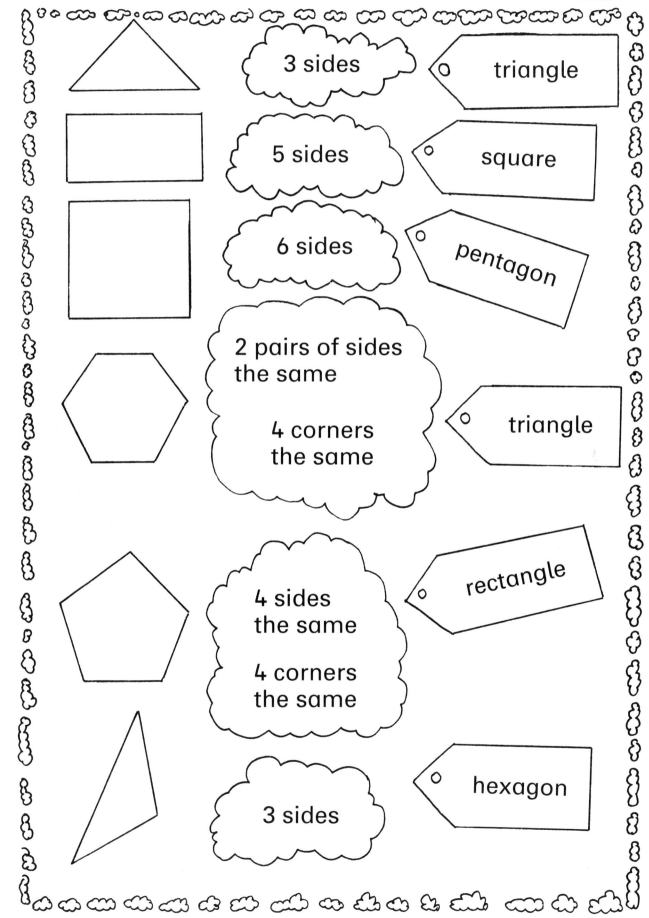

Shape match – board

corners all same	4 corners	sides all same	4 sides	square	 □
corners all same	4 corners	pairs of sides same	4 sides	rectangle	 ▭
			6 sides	hexagon	⬡
			5 sides	pentagon	⬠
			3 sides	triangle	△

Shape match – cards

corners all same	4 corners	sides all same	4 sides	square	☐
corners all same	4 corners	pairs of sides same	4 sides	rectangle	▭
			6 sides	hexagon	⬡
			5 sides	pentagon	⬠
			3 sides	triangle	△

Cubes and cuboids

These are all cuboids
Colour them
Ring the cubes

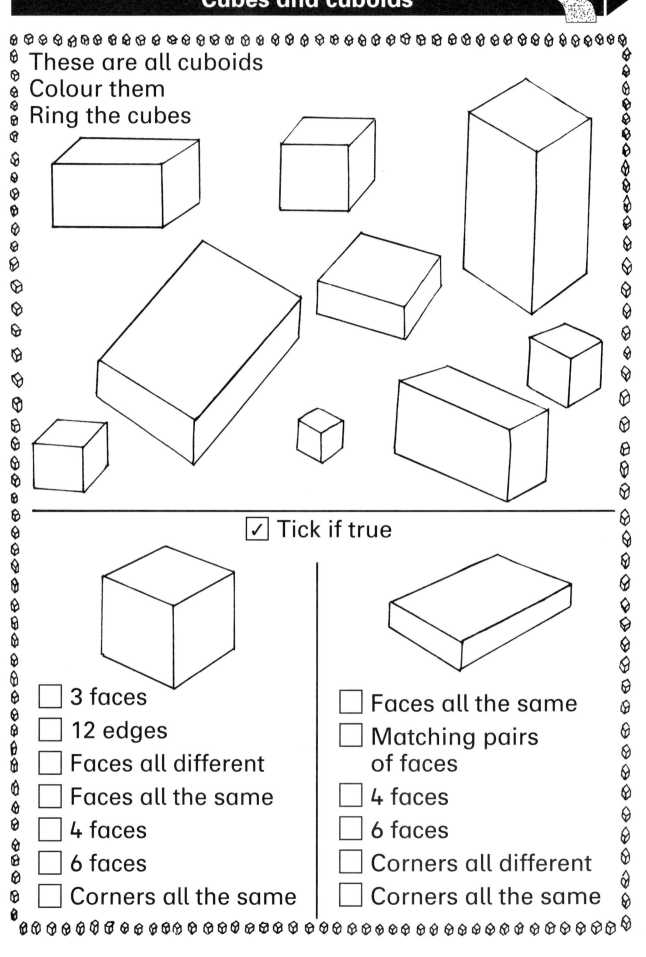

✓ Tick if true

☐ 3 faces
☐ 12 edges
☐ Faces all different
☐ Faces all the same
☐ 4 faces
☐ 6 faces
☐ Corners all the same

☐ Faces all the same
☐ Matching pairs of faces
☐ 4 faces
☐ 6 faces
☐ Corners all different
☐ Corners all the same

Cylinders

Draw a cylinder

Draw a cylinder cut open and laid flat

Colour the cylinders

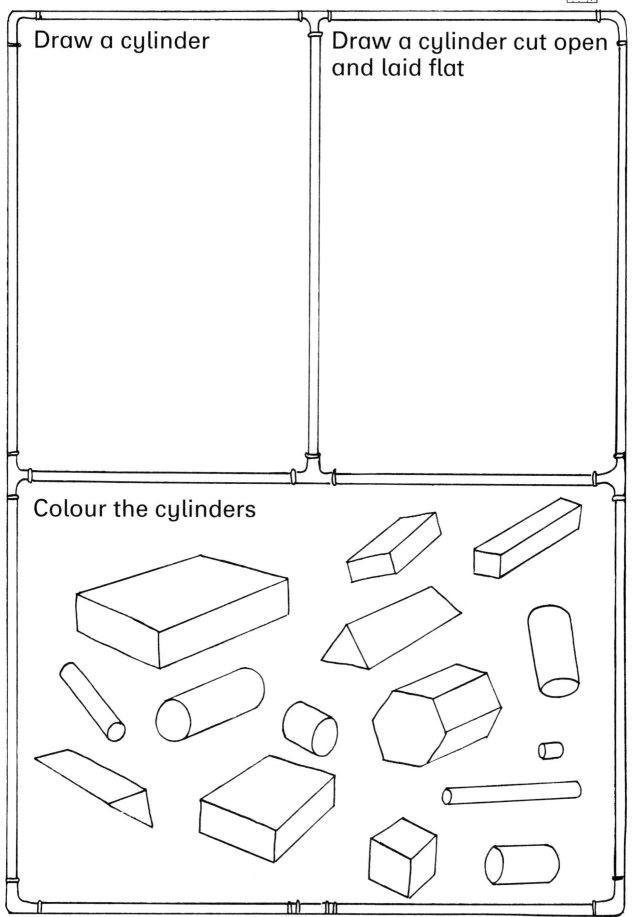

3-D shape game – base boards

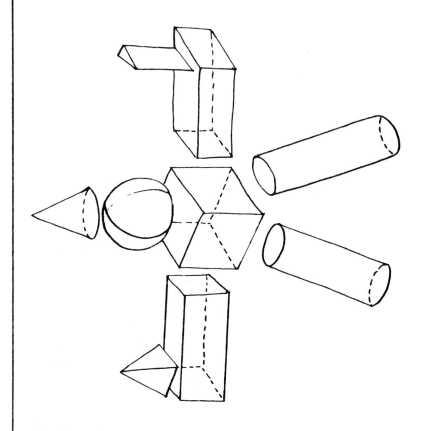

Collect 9 shape cards
to make this model

cuboid – 2   cube – 1
sphere – 1   cylinder – 2
triangular prism – 1
cone – 1   pyramid – 1

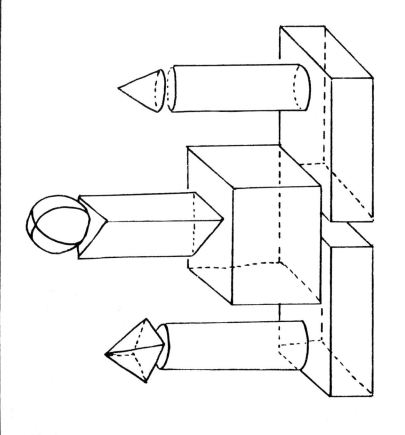

Collect 9 shape cards
to make this model

cuboid – 2   cube – 1
sphere – 1   cylinder – 2
triangular prism – 1
cone – 1   pyramid – 1

3-D shape game – base boards

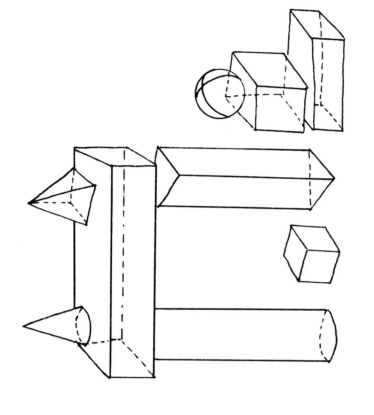

Collect 9 shape cards
to make this model

cuboid – 2   cube – 2
sphere – 1   cylinder – 1
triangular prism – 1
cone – 1   pyramid – 1

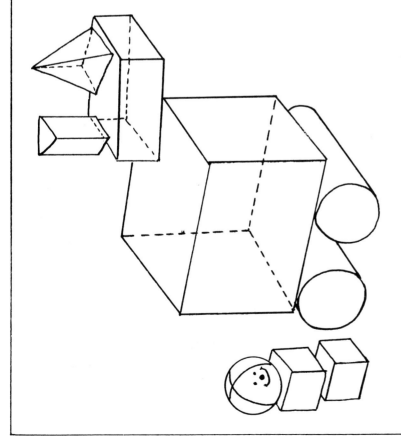

Collect 9 shape cards
to make this model

cuboid – 2   cube – 2
sphere – 1   cylinder – 2
triangular prism – 1
pyramid – 1

3-D shape game – cards

Right angles

Draw the things you see with right angles

Mark the right angles

How many can you find?

Shapes with right angles

Circle the right angles

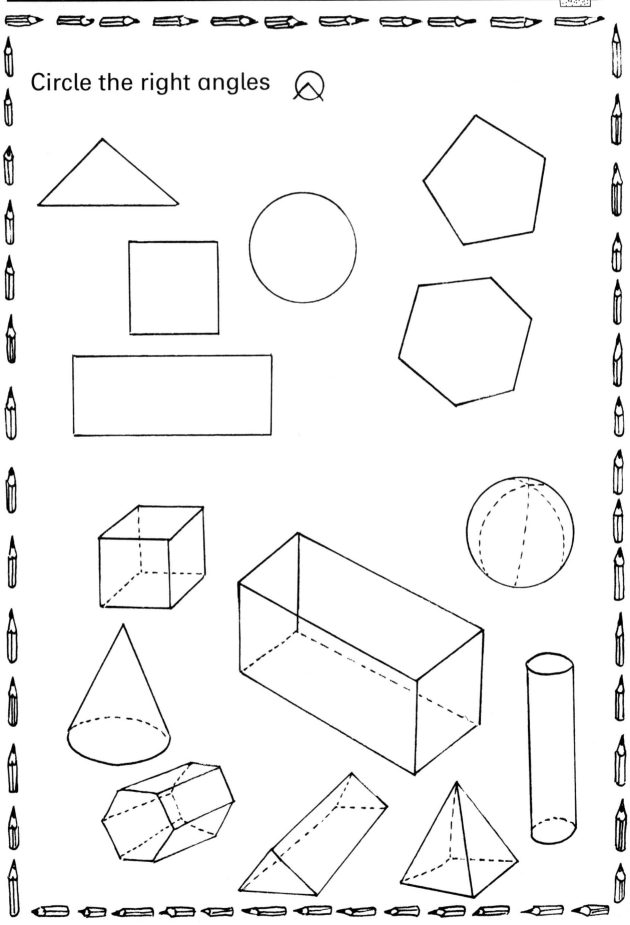

Angles around school

Look for angles like these	Where are they? Draw or write

Shape characters and play titles

Mr Cube   Mrs Cuboid   Little Triangle   Little Square   Little Rectangle

Make up your own characters
What can you call your play?

The Shape Family goes Camping
or
Mr Cube's Bad Day
or ...

Draw your shape family here

2-D shapes quiz

Do you know about shapes?

What can you say about a triangle?

_____

_____

Name the shape with 6 sides _____

What shape has 4 sides the same and
4 corners the same? _____

Name this shape _____

What shape has 5 sides? _____

Name this shape _____

These words will help you

circle   rectangle   hexagon   pentagon   square

3-D shapes quiz

A die is a _____

A ball is a _____

Telescopes are shaped like _____

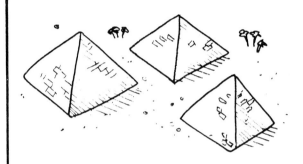

The Egyptians built the _____

This shape is a

_____

This shape is a

_____

This shape is a

_____

This shape is a _____

cuboid   cube   triangular prism   cone   sphere   hexagonal prism
pyramid   cylinder

2-D shapes and symmetry

Colour the symmetrical shapes

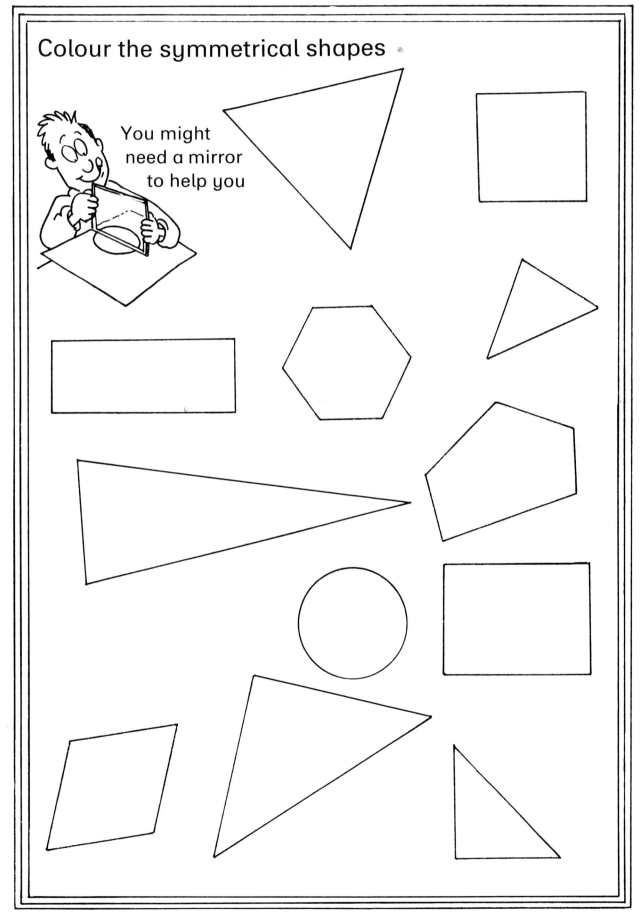

You might need a mirror to help you

House number symmetry

The number on _____ house is _____

Draw the number again.
Make the number so big
it nearly fills the page!

Check the numerals

Are they symmetrical?

Letter symmetry

My name is _____

Draw your name, making the letters large
Tick the letters that are symmetrical

Planes of symmetry

Write in how many planes of symmetry each shape has

Points of the compass

Draw and decorate the points of the compass

Have you made your drawing look really good?

Compass trail

Start

Try not to make this too hard for your friends!

Keep the trail to the parts of school that your teacher says are OK to use

Finish

Clockwise and anti-clockwise

Which way round? Write clockwise or anti-clockwise.

Mapping

Give each drink a straw

☐ drinks

☐ straws

Give each stick a toffee apple

☐ sticks

☐ toffee apples

Give each woman a mouth

☐ women

☐ mouths

Give each kite a string

☐ kites

☐ strings

Complex mapping

Match lambs to ewes

Match shoes to feet

Match wheels to cars

Weather frequency table

Weather ... a 20 day study

Key

sunny day

cloudy day

rainy day

	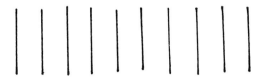

Frequency data collection

Key

What you are looking for

How many times it happens

Customer frequency table

Day of week	Number of customers between 9 o'clock and 10 o'clock		
	TV	Flowers	Fruit
Monday	I	III	II
Tuesday	II	IIIII	IIII
Wednesday	III	IIII	IIIIII
Thursday	I	II	IIIIII
Friday	IIIII	IIIIIIIII	IIIIIIIIII
Saturday	IIII	IIIIIIII	IIIIIIIII

Graph axes and grid

C98

Problem cards for block graphs or bar charts

Find out what your classmates' favourite meals are

Find out your classmates' shoe sizes

What pets do your classmates have?

Find out your classmates' favourite colours

Shopping list and index

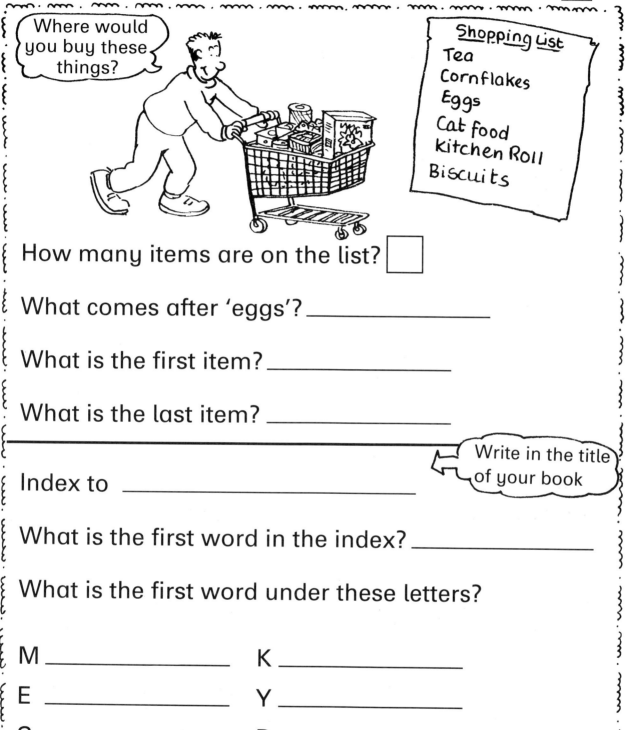

How many items are on the list? ☐

What comes after 'eggs'? _____

What is the first item? _____

What is the last item? _____

Index to _____

Write in the title of your book

What is the first word in the index? _____

What is the first word under these letters?

M _____   K _____

E _____   Y _____

S _____   D _____

What is the last word in the index? _____

What letters of the alphabet have *no* entries in the index? _____

Pictograms

How many girls in a class?

Key 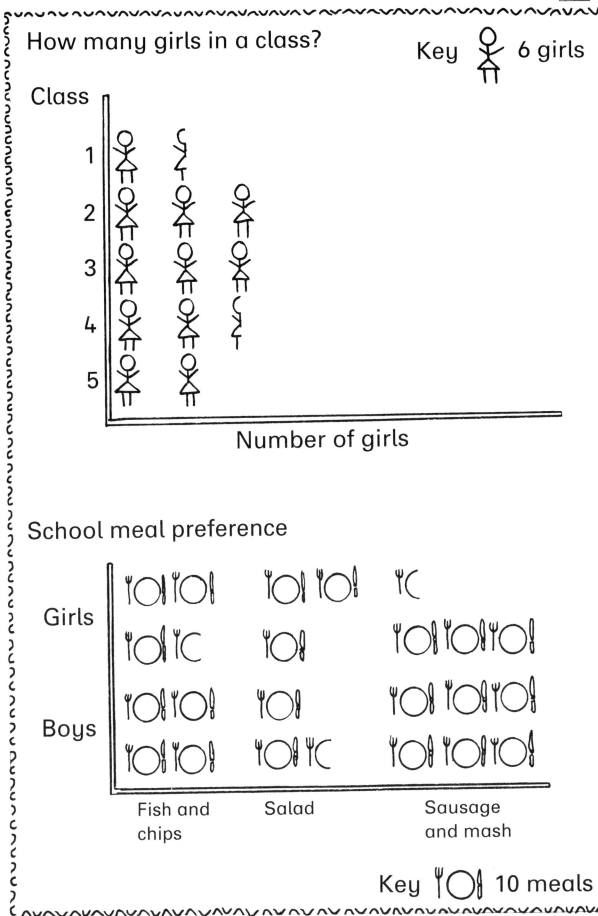 6 girls

School meal preference

Key ⌡⃝⃒ 10 meals

Pictograms

Favourite cartoon characters

Key ☆ 2 people

Age

7

6

5

Mickey Mouse   Bug's Bunny   Tom and Jerry   Pink Panther

Does it rain more often on Mondays?

Key ☁ 2 days

Weather

Sun

Rain

Mon   Tue   Wed   Thur   Fri

Chance happenings

What is the chance of these things happening?

The sun will shine tomorrow.

I will find a meteorite in my garden today.

My house will move to the other side of the street while I am at school tomorrow.

Mum will forbid me to wash for a week.

My feet will grow 2 sizes before Christmas.

I shall watch TV in the next 2 days.

The school holidays will end.

I shall have tea at a friend's house soon.

I shall paint a picture in the next two weeks.

Record sheet

Pupil's name _____

AT2 Number	1 Level 1	2	3	4
	5	6	7	8
	9	10	11	12
	13	14 Level 2	15	16
	17	18	19	20
	21	22	23	24
	25	26 Level 3	27	28
	29	30	31	32
	33	34	35	36
	37	38	39	40
	41	42	43	44
	45	46	47	48
	49	50 Level 1	51	52 Level 2
AT3 Algebra	53	54	55	56
	57	58	59 Level 3	60
	61	62	63	64
	65	66	67 Level 1	68
AT4 Shape and space	69	70	71	72 Level 2
	73	74	75	76
	77	78	79	80
	81	82	83	84
	85 Level 3	86	87	88
	89	90	91	92
AT5 Handling data	93 Level 1	94	95 Level 2	96
	97	98	99	100 Level 3
	101	102	103	

Spinners

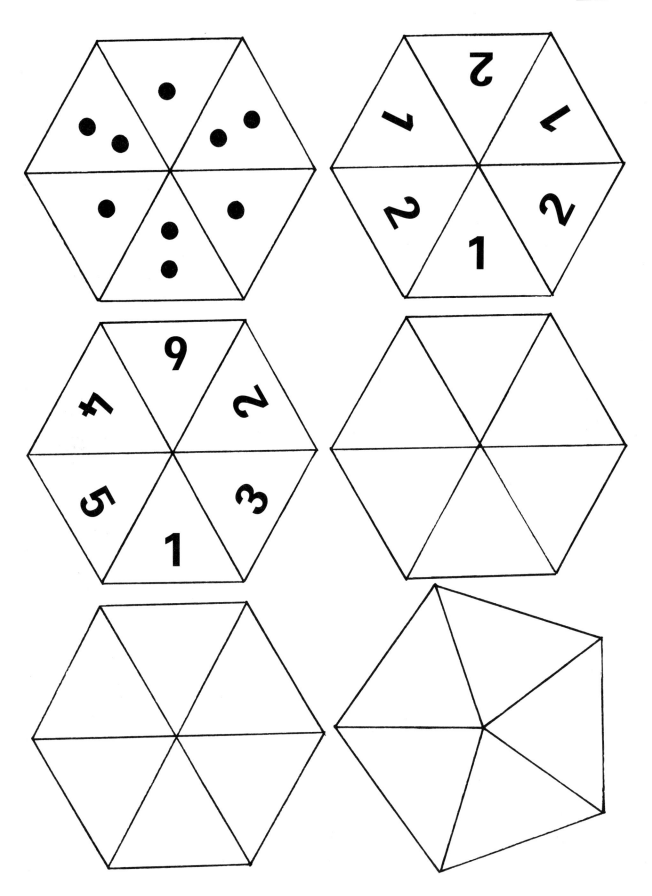

Hundred squares

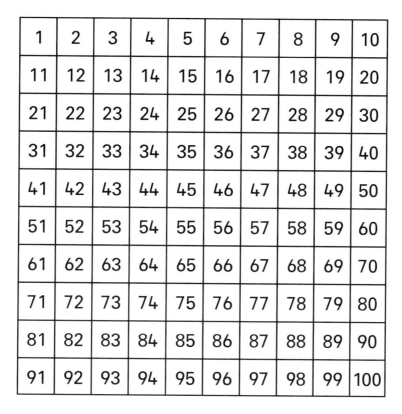

1	2	3	4	5	6	7	8	9	10
11	12	13	14	15	16	17	18	19	20
21	22	23	24	25	26	27	28	29	30
31	32	33	34	35	36	37	38	39	40
41	42	43	44	45	46	47	48	49	50
51	52	53	54	55	56	57	58	59	60
61	62	63	64	65	66	67	68	69	70
71	72	73	74	75	76	77	78	79	80
81	82	83	84	85	86	87	88	89	90
91	92	93	94	95	96	97	98	99	100

Large hundred square

1	2	3	4	5	6	7	8	9	10
11	12	13	14	15	16	17	18	19	20
21	22	23	24	25	26	27	28	29	30
31	32	33	34	35	36	37	38	39	40
41	42	43	44	45	46	47	48	49	50
51	52	53	54	55	56	57	58	59	60
61	62	63	64	65	66	67	68	69	70
71	72	73	74	75	76	77	78	79	80
81	82	83	84	85	86	87	88	89	90
91	92	93	94	95	96	97	98	99	100

Large squares

Small squares

Dotty squares

Dotty triangles

Venn diagram: two discrete sets

Draw or list your sets here

Venn diagram: four discrete sets

These are for your sets

Venn diagram: two overlapping sets

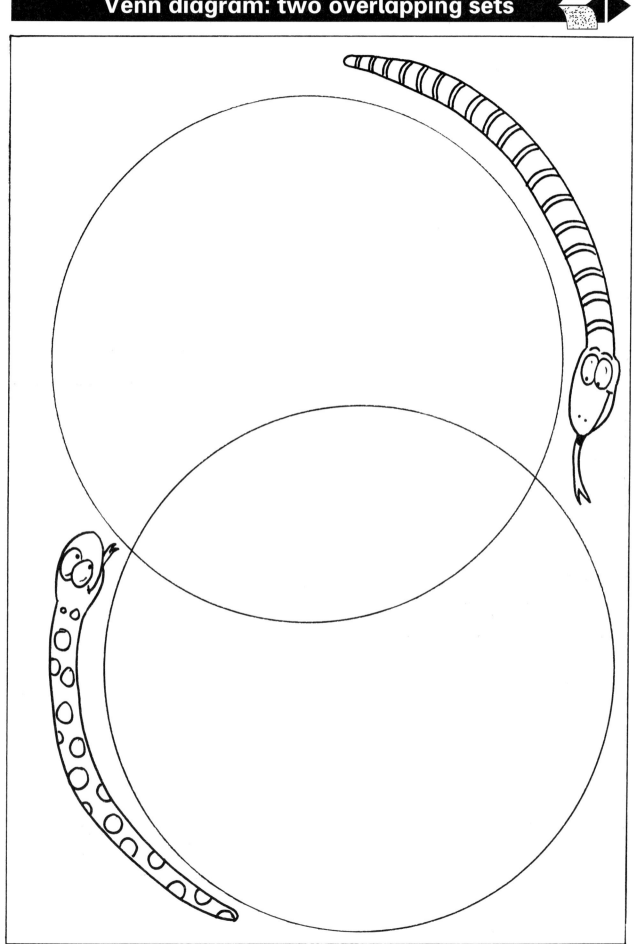

Carroll diagram